WOUNDED IN THE CHURCH THERE'S HEALING FOR THE WOUNDED

Revelation 22:2

BY EVANGELIST LENA MAE WILLIS

Copyright © 2004 by Evangelist Lena Mae Willis

Wounded In The Church
by Evangelist Lena Mae Willis

Printed in the United States of America

ISBN 1-594674-27-2

All rights reserved solely by the author. The author guarantees all contents are original and do not infringe upon the legal rights of any other person or work. No part of this book may be reproduced in any form without the permission of the author. The views expressed in this book are not necessarily those of the publisher.

Unless otherwise indicated, Bible quotations are taken from the Key Word Study Bible, King James Version. Copyright © 1984 and 1991.

www.xulonpress.com

Acknowledgments

This little book is written from my heart by the inspiration of God; my prayer and hope is that, in some way, it will help restore our daughters who have been wounded in the church. First of all, I would like to dedicate this book to my entire family, especially, my husband, James, "my Babe", the best husband in the world. Thank you, honey for your encouraging words, while I sat up, sometimes, all night writing. To my daughters, all six of you, Jerry, Mary Ann, Bobbie, Betty, Gertrude, Jamesetta, and James,Jr., Ronnie and Alice, my extended children. To my sisters whom I love very much, Mary Oneatha (deceased) and Mary Ann Peace. My Church Family, Faith Temple Church of God in Christ. To the Revival Fellowship District Family. I love you all very much. Thank you, Dorothy, Rose Victorene and Mother Rosa. My brother Pastor Claudell Huey and my sister and greatest friend, Willette. A special thanks to all those persons whose words, songs, messages and scriptures that I borrowed from, thank you. A special thanks to my two extended nieces, Liz and Shelene, who encouraged me to keep writing. Thank you Clarence for your support; you are a real friend and you are always in my prayers. Finally, a grateful thanks to the two very special people who are responsible for the printing of my book. God bless you both, you know who you are.

Table of Contents

Acknowledgments		v
Introduction		ix
One	WHAT HAVE WE DONE?	13
Two	MR. TALL, DARK, AND HANDSOME	17
Three	SOMEBODY IS PRAYING FOR YOU	21
Four	A MESSAGE TO THE MOTHERS	25
Five	LAY ASIDE THE PAST	31
Six	JESUS CARES FOR YOU	35
Seven	WHAT ABOUT OUR SONS?	39
Eight	DON'T BE AN APPROVAL JUNKIE	41
Nine	MENDING OUR RELATIONSHIPS	45
Ten	THE BLESSINGS OF THE LORD	49
Eleven	THERE'S A BALM FOR YOU	53
Twelve	PASSING THE BATON	57
Thirteen	IT'S NOT AN OUTSIDE NEED; IT'S AN INSIDE NEED	63
Fourteen	PROMOTION COMES FROM GOD	67
Fifteen	IT'S PRAYING TIME	71

Introduction

While the title of the book seems to be a paradox, it is truly a reality in the church world today. We find that more and more people are testifying to the fact that they have been wounded in the church, that they have found no solace in the church for their situations or circumstances, that they find themselves holding on to pains for years and years, smiling on the outside but crying on the inside, attending church Sunday after Sunday, leaving the same way they came. It seems as if we have so many issues within the church that we have neglected the ministry that Christ has given us. 2 Corinthians 5:18 tells us that ". . . all things are of God, who hath reconciled us to himself by Jesus Christ and hath given us the ministry of reconciliation;"[1] but we haven't been able to bring the lost to Christ because we are finding ourselves lost in the church house. It seems as if the cries of wounded soldiers are going out, but no one is answering the call. As we look at our world today, we find the national media exposing the "dirty laundry" of the church. Leaders of churches are found guilty of moral sins; church organizations have fallen due to financial compromise; churches are cold and dormant because of spiritual compromise. We have churches full of people and not people full of the church. II Chronicles 7:14 states:

> *"If my people which are called by my name would humble themselves and pray, seek my face, turn from their wicked ways, then will I hear from heaven; I will forgive their sin and heal their land."*[2]

Saints, we must change! The same place where injury is inflicted, healing can be found. Jeremiah 8:22 says, "Is there no balm in Gilead; is there no physician there? Why then is not the health of the daughter of my people recovered?"[3] Jesus came to heal every ailment that afflicts us. "He healeth the broken in heart and bindeth up their wounds." (Psalms 147:3)[4] Jesus is calling us to pray. If we pray, hearts will be mended; if we pray, minds will be restored; if we pray, the saints' spirit will be lifted; if we pray, love will be renewed; if we pray, healing will be manifested.

As you read this biographical account of a woman of God, you will find encouragement in knowing that healing can and will take place. You will find yourself challenged to change according the will of God; you will find yourself looking at your circumstance and confronting it saying to yourself, "I can do all through Christ which strengtheneth me" (Philippians 4:13).[5] You will find yourself understanding that we need each other and we should exhort one another to love. It is hoped that this book will leave you with at least one of two things: a mind to help in the healing of your brother or sister, or the courage to allow God to heal you.

Throughout this biographical account, there are problems discussed that are found in the church interspersed with encouragement and solutions. In chapter one, a vivid account of the problems in the church created by the people of God is discussed. It opens by giving a description of an individual who has been instructed on how to live a holy life, has been obedient to that lifestyle and has been wounded because of her lifestyle. In chapter two, the author shares an account of the struggles found in meeting the right mate. Chapter three offers encouragement to the reader letting them know that they are not alone. In Chapter four, the author speaks to the mothers of the church and challenges them to look at their approaches to the younger generation. Then in chapter five and six, the younger generation is challenged to forgive because help is coming their way through our Lord and Savior Jesus Christ. Jesus said, in Matthew 28:20b, "Lo, I am with you always even unto the end of the world. Amen."[6] He will never leave us regardless to whoever else leaves. Jesus will always be there.

In chapter seven, the sons of the church are addressed because not only are the daughters of the church being wounded, many of our sons are suffering hurt, as well. In chapter eight, the pressure to be a people pleaser is discussed. The author shares her experience in trying to conform to the whims of people and how it proved to be fruitless. In Ephesians 6:6, Paul tells us to do service, but "not with eyeservice, as menpleasers; but as servants of Christ, doing the will of God from the heart;"[7]. If we are doing service from the heart, this is all that matters. Chapter nine discusses the need for relationship building and chapter ten shows us the beauty and the blessings that can come from relationship, specifically the relationship between and man and woman. Chapter eleven comforts the reader to know that the Lord has healing for each one of us, but we must be willing to receive His healing.

In the last four chapters, the author discusses and exhorts both the older and younger generations. These last four chapters illustrate the tools needed to bridge the "so-called" gap between the generations. In chapter twelve, once again, the author addresses the older generation sharing with them the assets found in teaching and passing on relative traditions to the younger generations. In chapter thirteen, she discusses that the problems the still persist is because an inside problem needs to be fixed. The outside actions are only a symptom of an inside problem. In chapter fourteen, she shares the reality of principles of promotion in the church and how we can become distracted by promotion when, in fact, it truly must come from God if the service is to be fruitful. Finally, in the final chapter, chapter fifteen, the author exhorts us to pray. We must pray if we expect the Lord to heal us, (both the young and old) and move us forward.

CHAPTER ONE

"What Have We Done?"

She's saved at an early age and taught to live a clean life, free and separated from sin. She's told to "follow peace with all men, holiness without which no man shall see the Lord." Yes, Hebrews 12:14[1] is what we told her to do; she tries hard to obey; she's taught not to have any "men friends" and when she truly lives by these rules, she gets wounded. The married sisters in the church don't want her around their husbands because they get jealous and think she wants their husbands, when, in actuality, they are the ones who told her to be faithful and be in church as much as possible. When she does this, they start talking and spreading malicious gossip. Oh how sad it is to see the things we have caused! This dilemma leaves her with no one to turn to for encouragement. She's left feeling like nobody cares and her only thought is "what's the use? Nobody cares!" She tries to live by "their" rules, she tries to love everybody, she goes to church faithfully and what is the conversation? They say, she is "looking for a man" or she is "after the pastor." If she travels alone, and doesn't spend anytime with a "brother", then "they" say she is "going to meet a man." If she takes another woman with her, "they" say she is a lesbian. Oh mothers what have we done to the young women in the church? We have wounded our daughters in the church with our judgmental thoughts. Matthew 7:1-2 says, "Judge not that ye be not judged. For with what judgment ye judge, ye shall be judged and with what measure ye mete, it shall be measured to you again."[2] Would you want this to be you? Think about it! To judge others is to condemn yourself according to Romans 2:1.[3]

Single or widowed daughters—not every woman is watching you to see if you will make a mistake because none of us are free from mistakes and faults. We ". . . all have sinned, and come short of the glory of God;" according to Romans 3:23.[4] Some of us have made many mistakes, but God forgave us and blessed us; He gave us another chance and blessed us with husbands, who are saved and walking with the Lord as well, and today, we are happily married. I am one of those mothers. Now let me tell you how you can get the victory over your situation. Hold your head up high and keep your eyes on Jesus. Don't let anything come between you and Him. Make Him first and foremost in your life and he will see you through those lonely days and those dark nights. Trust Him for all your needs. Matthew 6:33 says, "But seek ye first the kingdom of God, and his righteousness; and all these [other] things shall be added unto you."[5] That means, husband, friends, money, whatever,

— It shall be given to you, but the best of all is that He will give you joy, hope, love, and peace. Don't ever doubt in your heart. That real peace comes **only** from God. That's why I encourage you to stay with Jesus because the safest place you have is in the arms of Jesus.

CHAPTER TWO

"Mr. Tall, Dark and Handsome"

Stop worrying about the arms of "Mr. Tall, Dark and Handsome" because it won't work. I already tried that. Be careful daughters. "Mr. Tall, Dark and Handsome will be sly and determined. After the Lord saved, my "Mr. Tall, Dark and Handsome" was so sure and determined that I would marry him because he was the pastor of a 1500 member church in another denomination. When I went to visit the church, I was received with so much love, and he said that I could really help him in his church. He was so sure of himself that he went out and bought me a one-karat engagement ring of which I put on a chain and wore around my neck, hidden, because I always felt condemned about wearing it. Even though I loved him, something did not feel right after God saved me. I talked with my pastor, who was my dad, Superintendent F. W. Cotton ever since I was a little girl. He was my friend; I loved to travel with him anywhere he went and he would let me go. My mother, "Ma Ma", Lena Joanna told me when I was one year old that Daddy took me with him in his brand new 1926 Model T Ford and while he was learning to drive, he hit his brakes and threw me out of the car (Ha, Ha, Ma Ma!), but I still kept going everywhere with my daddy. The point was that there was nothing that I wouldn't discuss or share with my Dad. We talked about everything. After God saved me and after talking to Daddy about "Mr. Tall, Dark and Handsome", I knew what I needed to do; I also knew it was going to be very difficult. Daddy's words were "if you want my advice, don't marry that fellow." That was his name for a guy he didn't care for, "that fellow." Dad told me, "he will draw you out of holiness and away from God." Needless to say, that was not the advice I wanted to hear because I was "in love." When you are in love or think you are, you don't always listen or hear the advice of someone who will tell you the truth. I began talking with the mothers in our church and they all prayed for me, all except for a few. You know, there always has to be a few. The gossip started; cold stares and strange looks followed. Some even told me, "don't get tangled up anymore or you will be sorry." But what I needed was an answer. Others just talked among themselves, gossiping about me. When people talk about you, especially those you confide in, It hurts, but keep a smile on your face and go to God for yourself; that's exactly what I did. The saints would tell you, in those days, when you had problems, to go on a three-day fast and just talk to God, seeking direction. To get my life back on track again, I sought God for three days and at the dawn of the last day, I had a **vision** from God. I was out in the San Francisco Bay standing on a foot-long log, fishing and I got a real strong bite. As I was beginning to try to reel the fish in, I would almost fall in the water backwards, but when I gave it some slack, I would almost fall in the water by being pulled forward, and I couldn't swim. So I said to myself, "I must turn this pole a loose." When I let the pole go, it went under the water and came back up to the surface. My fish had "Mr. Tall, Dark, and Handsome's" face on the hook. Suddenly, the log filled up with saints from my home church and as I tried to tell them what was on my hook they said, "we know; that's why we came for you." As I watched his face, I felt helpless, but they walked me to safe ground."

CHAPTER THREE

"Somebody is Praying for You"

Listen daughters, you are not alone. Somebody is praying for you, and "with God all things are possible" (Matthew 19:26b).[6] I felt the pain for months. Oh yes, it hurts to give up someone you love, who loves you back. Remember nobody loves you like Jesus even when we don't love him. That day, I gave up "Mr. Tall, Dark and Handsome," who was paying my rent, buying my clothes, doing nice things for my two daughters, giving us anything we wanted. All that was wonderful, but God had saved me, filled me with the Holy Ghost, (Thank you, Lord!) and I gave it all up. I walked away with nothing of earthly goods, so I could gain the best part of my life, a life with Christ. I started shopping at the Goodwill, the Next to New Shoppe, and the Second Chance Store, but I had peace. For almost a year, I hurt so bad I thought I would die each day. I could feel the pain in my heart, yet again, I listened to the voice of God and he brought me out and gave me the victory.

I prayed daily for God to help me smile and He gave me a sense of humor about my bad times in life. During my early life, I weighed only ninety-nine pounds and was given the name "Skinny." My nose was large, so I used my sense of humor to lighten and brighten my view on life. Daughters, I'm sharing some of my fears and hurts in the church to say to, once again, you are not alone. "Mr. Tall, Dark, and Handsome" showed me his true side after I told him that I could not marry him. After having that vision and telling him about it, he cursed and said bad things about the saints in my church; he accused me of telling them my business and said that they were "jealous" of me "getting a good husband." I tried to explain that it was God's will, but he didn't have enough God to even try to understand the will of God. Don't be fooled by "Mr. Tall, Dark, and Handsome"; you may think that he's the one when all the while he is "a wolf in sheep's clothing." After that conversation, I could feel the pain in my heart for months; it hurt so badly. I just felt like I would not be able to go on without him, so, once again, I went on a fast asking God to please help me. Again, I prayed daily for God to help me smile again and God continued developing my sense of humor. When I laughed with others, it was expressing a joy that moved out the pain from the depths of my soul, and it touched others, giving them gladness. God ". . . will fill your mouth with laughter and your lips with joyful shouting" (Job 8:21).[7] Daughters, you may have been wounded, but there's healing going through you right now as you read this (Jeremiah 33:6).[8] So, don't give up because our God yet reigns; listen to God and in your heart, "in all thy ways, acknowledge him, and he shall direct thy paths" (Proverbs 3:6).[9] Daughters, keep your self-respect, your self-esteem, and don't settle for anything that is not worthy of you. Remember my sense of humor began with me having the nickname of "Skinny" because I only weighed ninety-nine pounds, was 5'6" tall, had a large nose and a small face, but my sense of humor kept me going. When someone said something about my nose, I could smile and say, "that's the way you identify a beautiful Cotton woman because we all have one." Daughters, keep your sense of humor, and believe in yourself. Yes, you have made mistakes; haven't we all, (maybe worse)? But remember, you are somebody, so don't settle for less. Everyday of your journey, try to learn something of value because life is a journey, and sometimes, we do wonder if we are making any progress. YES, YOU ARE! So live one day at a time and enjoy each day because there are blessings around every corner awaiting your discovery. I am telling myself "stay on the wheel" because it just may be God's will. Sometimes God has to break us to make us, but He is faithful and just. If we confess our sins, He will forgive us (1John 1:9).[10] The world is unjust; it will accuse you, abuse you, use you, misuse you, and then loose you. Oh, but there is another side: Jesus will choose you, pick you up, clean you up and use you. Daughters, be used by God. I know you feel like this is only happening to you, but that's not the truth. Our church family has wounded many of us because somebody told us to just keep it to ourselves and tell God about it, so we did because we were made to think we were weak in the faith if we asked for help to find a solution to our problem. The Word of God was the answer: "confess your faults one to another. . ." (James 5:16a).[11] Pray until God, by His Spirit, leads you to someone who will be a friend and mother to you. Don't let anything or anybody make you feel ashamed about your mistakes. We all have made some at one time or another. Remember God is a forgiving God. My mother "Ma Ma Lena Joanna" taught us: "Because you fall down, you don't have to lay there and wallow in it; get up, brush yourself off and start over again." Remember God allows U-turns anywhere, at anytime on this road, but when you make your turn just be sure it is a right turn onto the Prayer Lane that leads you all the way to Bible Reading Avenue. Don't forget to make a right turn onto Fasting Boulevard, which will allow you to make a right turn onto Confession Drive. Then, go right into Praising God Expressway. Yes Lord! Praise God for what He's done, for what He's doing, for what He will do; praise Him for who He is and stay faithful to God no matter what.

CHAPTER FOUR

A Message to the Mothers

Mothers, we all stumble in many ways. Our young daughters need to know this about us; they need models and they need insight that is helpful, not harmful. Unfortunately, some of us older women forget what it was like to go through our young days in the church. Sometimes rather than easing the burden of anxiety and guilt, we add toil by not letting the young women know we experienced the same emotions. We hide our faults by telling our daughters not to feel what they are feeling, giving them the impression that some people don't experience those types of feelings. First of all, mothers you cannot stop a person's feelings by telling them not to feel that way. Second, it doesn't help to give the impression that these feelings are abnormal, and finally, it is dishonest for an older woman to give the impression that she never had these difficulties when, indeed, we all have and some of us still do. Yes, mothers, we need to take a good look at our life and see what kind of model we are to the younger women so we can teach our daughters to look for an older woman who can serve as a guiding model and interpreter. Daughter ask the Lord to direct you to that kind of person; He will: He did it for me. **Warning:** it is easy to get our eyes off Jesus Christ and on people who will disappoint us; remember that. Not all older women who appear to have it together spiritually and emotionally actually do; just remember that no human being is perfect. Sometimes the person who is the most honest about their imperfections can be the most help; it is important for us to realize that only Jesus Christ is the same yesterday, today and forever (Hebrews 13:8).[12] Flesh will fail you!

Mothers, who are First ladies or Pastors' Wives, (the title that I like to call you) learn who you are so you can be the real, true influence in your husband's church. Show love for every woman in the church whether she is married, single, widowed, young, middle-aged, or old; everybody needs a hug. It's time for us to change our attitude if we ever intend to help our children, not just our biological and spiritual children, but also the children of the world. Mothers, our daughters are hurting, sitting in the church beside us; it's time for us to remember we were once young and hurting. Let us stop complaining about what used to be and pray until we feel the pain; then, the church will start seeing the gain.

Mothers, our day is not over: it has just begun! I learned through my pain and suffering how to help our daughters. Please let's stop using the words "they didn't do that in my day." Well, we didn't wear sequin suits, but we wear them now. We couldn't stay in five-star hotels "in that day", but we do now! Thank God for this day; it's time to kill "Couldn't, Can't, and usta" and pray until we become impregnated by God with "I can do all things through Christ which strengtheneth me" (Philippians 4:13).[13]

Mothers and Sisters, we can't erase what's already taken place, so let's be a light for our daughters to see it right. Oh Lord, let the light of thy presence shine through us to influence others to follow thee and Lord give us your spirit of sympathy and love and free us from unkind criticism.

We have lost so many of young people because we have not used wisdom. We have been too critical, too judgmental, too accusing until we have caused our daughters to turn to lesbian relationships because we've said it's a sin to have a man friend when we should have been teaching them how to go about being respected by a man. Don't blame our youth for their attitude. They are only doing what they see us do. We have no respect for each other; we talk about each other in the presence of our youth, so mothers, what do we expect? We have driven our youth away. We have the best singers, the best missionaries, the best preachers, the best organists, but yet we sit in our services with empty choir stands, no music, and no young preachers in our churches. Mothers and Fathers, ask yourselves why are our youth leaving? Where are they going? Let's stop worrying about their outside and try to get something on their insides; let's come together and take a good look and we will find that it's not how they dress. Don't get me wrong: I know the Bible says to dress "in modest apparel"(I Timothy 2:9)[14]; I also know that the Bible says "therefore if any man be in Christ, he is a new creature; old things are passed away, behold all things become new" (2 Corinthians 5:17),[15] so let's pray for a new birth, for our youth, for a new attitude, for our relationships with our young people. Mothers, if we as mothers give birth to a natural baby that has some deformities, do we leave them at the hospital? No, we bring them home and love them and we even find time to show more love so they will never feel unloved. We must do the same thing for our spiritual babies, so they won't feel unloved by us. We need them; the church needs young people, both men and women. Mothers and sisters, get yourself in a place with God, where you can feel the cares of the women in your surroundings. I can't say it enough. We should not be ashamed to share our faults and crazy actions we did as young women. I remember that I would race a car with anybody, and, at that time, you were considered a "chicken" if you didn't take a dare. Driving a car, walking around with "a chip on your shoulder" and daring anybody to knock it off were part of my faults. See I had been hurt, so I wanted to hurt back, but daughters, that's not the answer. Mothers, we must pray for an answer for our daughters.

We have many adults in this day struggling with the pain of molestation that they experienced in the church as a child. Mothers we must stop looking the other way, pretending this can't happen in the church, that if we pray, it will just go away. I Won't! We must expose the devil: silence is still public enemy number one. Molestation and Sexual abuse that is kept secret is like puss oozing from a wound. The image and the thought of this are not pleasant, but it must happen in order for healing to come. Mothers, we are living in an evil day; we need more churches with ministries that openly teach on spousal abuse, sexual abuse and child abuse. It's been a dark and ugly secret for many years in the church, but it's time for us as mothers to break the silence and start addressing the ugly secrets in our lives. Stop looking the other way! Help our daughters by exposing the devil openly. These things have been kept quiet too long. Our daughters need to know. They are not beyond help or healing because they have made mistakes and have gotten wounded in the church. Pray that the Holy Ghost will reveal the areas where you need healing and allow the Holy Ghost to release you from memories of the things that have happened to you in the past and start looking toward the future then pray for strength to forgive the ones who wounded you and finally realize that forgiveness does not mean that what happens to you wasn't wrong, but the Bible teaches us to "love our enemies." Read Matthew 5:44[16] and Matthew 6:14-15.[17] Daughters, you must get past your pain and hurts or it will always be there with you. Young ladies, be careful where you go and who you go with. Mother Welch says and teaches all the time to " be careful whom you take with you." It's time for us as older mothers to pray for some wisdom, more insight and recognize that these problems exist in the church. We must start teaching our young women that it's not only men molesters: there are lesbians also in the church who will try and trap our daughters.

CHAPTER FIVE

Lay Aside the Past

Daughters, I haven't forgotten about Mr. "Tall, Dark, and Handsome", but I believe that it is imperative that you understand you shouldn't go too fast living for God; this life takes time and patience. If I had not stayed with God, I wouldn't have had this experience and this information to share with you in this little book. Experience is our best teacher. God allowed me to go through this, so I would be able to help others lay aside the past and look to the future. I found it's not good to live in the past; some of my past is full of its burdens, heartaches and pains of many, many years. For several years, I carried these burdens of hurt and shame wanting to share them but not knowing who I could share them with, but I found out burdens carried from the past affect us in the present. We can't change the past, but we must deal with it honestly to truly lay it aside. Psalms 142[18] tells us that David was deeply troubled by people who were hurting him. Listen to these words as you read it;

mark the things that touch your heart, and see how David dealt with his feelings before the Lord. David was open with God.

Then, Read Psalm 32.[19] Coming out of denial about some of my problems has freed me from much pain. God is the same with everyone; He has no respect of person. He can and will free you from your burdens and pain from the past. Read Psalm 116.[20] As we lay aside the past, we will begin to heal and see life from God's point of view. Lay aside pleasing people and understand that pleasing God involves the loss of our agenda; don't live for people's approval. St. John 12:42-43[21] provides an example of people yielding to peer pressure. Don't worry about the praise of men; live as Paul did: ". . .free from all men. . ." (I Corinthians 9:19)[22] and empty yourself of all your own things in order to depend on God for everything. Don't depend on self for anything because the greatest burden we have to carry in life is self. The most difficult thing we have to manage is self. In laying down our burdens, the first one to get rid of is self; then, we will be in a place with God spiritually where we will be able to help others. It is our responsibility to restore each other; Paul tells us in Galatians 6:1, "Brethren, if a man be overtaken in a fault, ye which are spiritual restore such an one in the spirit of meekness."[23]; make sure you watch yourself because it could be you; stop looking at the speck of sawdust in your sister's or daughter's eye and pay more attention to the plank in your own eye. First, we must move the plank from our eyes and then we can see clearly to remove the speck from the eyes of others. "Can the blind lead the blind? Shall they both not fall into the ditch?" (Luke 6:39-42).[24]

Mothers, we must be completely humble and gentle, patient and bearing with one another in love (Ephesians 4:2).[25] Work hard at bearing with one another; let us make every effort to keep the unity among ourselves (Ephesians 4:2-3).[26] Sisters and Mothers, let's ask ourselves a question and see how we stand: how do we view younger women in Leadership positions in the church? Do we respect them and honor them as fellow members of Christ's body or do we feel we are more important than they are because we are older, and have been saved longer? Do we insist on doing things the way we used to? No, we must encourage one another and build each other up. I Thessalonians 5:11 lets us know that the old and the young must edify one another.[27] Let us take Paul as our example when He wrote to Timothy. He was not jealous or envious, but he showed him love and gave Him advice and instructions. He charged this young man to preach the Word, to be prepared in season and out of season, to correct, rebuke, and encourage with careful instruction (2 Tim. 4:2).[28] That's what we must do for our daughters: love them, teach them and involve them in the work of the Lord and you will be surprised how valuable they can be in the work, Mothers. If you lay the past aside, you can make friends for life, friends who will love you and help you. I have many sons and daughters, but these are friends who I can share any problem with and they are much younger then I. Sometimes, I feel myself getting mushy when I think about it. I have to pray and ask the Lord to help me to concentrate on Him; I need to listen to the voice of the Lord, so I can continue to give Godly instructions not from "Lena Mae" but from God. So, Wake Up Mothers! Our young women are very much needed. They will be your hands, your feet, and your mouth.

CHAPTER SIX

Jesus Cares for You

In these pages, I want to express to you that many women in the church, sometimes, feel that no one cares, but know that Jesus cares and so do many of the mothers. We have walked in your shoes, but as I said before, we were taught to keep it to ourselves, so no one could make us feel weak or ashamed about our problems. We were told to build a better relationship with our family and our church family and share our hurts and mistakes with them. I can't say it enough: there are women all over the church world who are abused daily by a spouse in the home, or their children are abused. Sometimes, they have an abusive boss at work or just false friends. You are not in a class by yourself. You are surrounded by "so great cloud of witnesses, so let us lay aside every weight and the sin which doth so easily beset us and let us run with patience the race that is set before us," (Hebrews 12:1).[29] The first thing we must do before starting the race is to do what the scripture tells us.

At this moment, I am remembering a message I heard in Memphis, Tennessee in the Church of God in Christ, Inc. Holy Convocation in November 2002. The preacher's subject was "Strip." I truly thank him for this message. He talked about how hurting sisters in the church would be wise to strip off the old self, which follows the former ways, get rid of bitterness and run with forgiveness. He said that these sisters needed to remove rage, as well as jealous and malicious insults "Be Careful for nothing; but in everything by prayer and supplication with thanksgiving. . . (Philippians 4:6-7a).[30] Give God the praise for everything. Learn to forgive those who you know have hurt you and those who have betrayed your trust, those who have taken the secrets you shared with them and used them against you. You can do it without holding any animosity in your heart; you can be like David and yet love. Yes, it hurts, but David shows us that it's possible. "Wickedness is in the midst thereof: deceit and guile depart not from her streets. For it was not an enemy that reproached me; than I could have borne it: neither was it he that hated me that did magnify himself against me; then I would have hid myself from him: But it was thou, a man mine equal, my guide and mine acquaintance. We took sweet counsel together and walked unto the house of God in company" (Psalms 55:11-14).[31] I had to forgive everything that had been done to me, and since I did, I have total forgiveness, freedom and joy in my spirit. Daughters, learn to lay aside anxiety and search for peace. I know from self-experience you can forgive and love someone who's wronged you. The Holy Ghost taught me how to forgive and get pass my hurts. First, I began laying aside bitterness and started running with forgiveness. Don't be ashamed to admit you have a need, mothers. Missionaries pray with our daughters and as they pray, listen with an open heart so you will be able to feel their hurts, pain and shame, begging God to set them free, saying to the Lord. "Please help me!" Mothers, sometimes our daughters are in lesbian relationships. When you hear them asking God to deliver them from these conditions, don't talk about them, don't repeat what you hear them admit, put your arms around them and show them a real love just like Jesus showed you. There are young women with many personal problems in all of our churches; there are some women sitting in our churches with problems that they don't know how to solve. Not long ago, I talked with a young lady who was hurting in her soul. All she needed was someone to listen to her. Mothers, there is another young lady somewhere and she needs you to show her some love, not rebuke. We have young women in our churches crying on the inside and we are so prone to sitting in church looking prim and proper, and acting like we have never done any wrong in our lives. Jesus just delivered us before we got caught. Now we have let ourselves become older women who are bitter; Bitterness is like cancer; it spreads all over you if it's not caught in time. Each heart knows it own bitterness; you try to ignore your own roots of bitterness hoping it will just go away if you don't talk about it. Sorry, sisters, it won't go away until you give it to Jesus. Not only are we bitter, we are mean, selfish, critical, falsely pious, and suspicious, yet we are saying that we are saved and filled with the Holy Ghost, testifying, "I want to be like Jesus." Well, mothers, our Lord was never suspicious, never bitter, and never in despair about anybody because He put God first— in trust. We need to do the same.

CHAPTER SEVEN

What About Our Sons?

While we have only considered our daughters and mothers, the Holy Ghost has spoken to my spirit about our sons. Like our daughters, we have sons that are in trouble and, fathers, they need you to give them some hope from your life; show them that every preacher is not a pimp and every pastor is not out just for money, a hot pink suit and a Cadillac. Show them a Godly man; let them know by your life that there are some shepherds who are not breeding the flock; you be the one who is feeding the flock. Let our young men know what life is about. For years, we have taught our daughters Titus 2:3.[32] Oh, but there is a Titus 2:2 first for the men and their sons. We, as mothers, know Titus 2:3, but it bears repeating for our Fathers: You, "aged men, be sober, grave, temperate, sound in faith, in charity, in patience",[33] that's your part, Fathers. My darling husband, James, taught me a song that we haven't sang in a long time, but it speaks so clearly and loudly to our mothers and fathers. The song says, "Let us run to Jesus everyone. Mothers bring your daughters. Fathers bring your sons and let us run to Jesus everyone. Because time is running out and we are running out of time."[34]

Take off the weights and start running; start looking for our young men and women. When you find them, put your arms around them and show them some love not criticism. Pray for them; don't talk about them. Our past mothers and fathers had enough power to pray out a whole membership, so surely we can pray for and obtain that same power for this day and this generation. We say this generation is rude, that they show no respect to us as seniors. Well, what do we expect, mothers and fathers? Have we taught them these things? Have we showed them by our life by respecting each other and showing compassion to each other? Have we been examples by obeying those who have rule over us? Each of us must ask ourselves this question and then answer it from our hearts. We can only feel our children's cares and admit it was us who let down and lowered the standards of holiness not our youth; they are doing what we have allowed to happen. Our yesterdays present some irreparable things to us. In other words, "some yesteryear opportunities can't be brought back." Those opportunities will never return, so let the past sleep, but let it sleep on the bosom of Jesus.

CHAPTER EIGHT

Don't Be an Approval Junkie

We must begin to work for God with our youth in mind and our hearts not worrying about what others will say or think; live for God's approval not man's. Do not let yourself become an "approval junkie" because you will live your life as a hostage to other people's opinions and judgments, making their thoughts and motives more important than those that God has given you. If you do, you will find yourself feeling their way and behaving their way. Approval seekers only look good: they have to. I know because I've been there, done that. I found out the hard way that people pleasing isn't Godly, nor is it spiritually healthy. Appeasers usually end up feeling used, unappreciated and driven to become all things to all people. They have to in order to maintain their image and to keep getting approval from people. It looks like they are giving you something, but that is not the case. Actually, you become a slave with a need to be admired. I have learned to seek to please God, not man. I am not in a friendship, kinship, or a popularity contest. Finding yourself in this place allows you to do the will of God freely. When you're an appeaser, you are never allowed to do the will of God freely. All I am saying, is stop being a people pleaser, so you will be free to get on with the life God has chosen for you; get rid of your fears of man. Some of us have great prayer lives, so we need to use them. Many churches that could help our young people are stifled and hindered by people pleasers and fear. Stop! Don't be bound any longer. There's freedom; I know what I am talking about. Today, as I write, I am delivered; I know there are many stumbling blocks, many hindrances in the way of young women. Many of you have two and three children, sometimes more, and it is hard being a single parent. I was a young, single woman with two beautiful daughters to raise by myself with a total income of two hundred and fifty dollars a month for three people. God made ways for my two daughters and myself. The people I worked for would send my girls to camp and pay for them. At school time, they would give me money to buy them some school clothes, and, at Christmas, we always got toys and gifts, both the girls and I. This all happened after I gave up my "Mr. Tall, Dark, and Handsome." Young daughters, if you stay with God, hold your head up high, He will bring you out as pure as gold. Then, tell God you will not settle for anything less than a B.M.W.—Black Man Working, filled with the Holy Ghost with somewhere to take you, not his Mama's house, with his own car to drive, not yours only. Everything that I am explaining to you is something I have been through; I gave up Mr. Tall, Dark and Handsome as well as his new Cadillac and rode the bus and I finally bought a station wagon that was so raggedy my daughters would hide in the back seat so their friends could not see them when they got to school. But because I stayed with God and didn't settle for what the devil had to offer, forty-five years later, God is yet blessing me.

CHAPTER NINE

Mending Our Relationships

So many mothers don't have connections with their biological daughters. When the Lord came for my oldest daughter, for one year, I had to watch my oldest daughter die slowly, and I had to give it over to God and accept His will; that's when I really understood the scripture Romans 8:28, " And we know that all things work together for good to them that love God, to them who are the called according to His purpose."[35] With my daughter dying, I couldn't see that bringing good, but the Lord spoke to my spirit and said, "If you love me, you will understand this." I simply said, "Thank you, Lord for everything; I know now it's for your purpose." Then, and only then, did God lift my burden and ease the pain, so you see my sisters, daughters and friends, you are not alone. Don't let the devil tell you nobody cares; somebody is praying for you and really knows what it feels like to be treated like it's a crime to be single or that every time you come in church somebody is looking at you strangely as if you are after someone's husband. I know how you feel, but you stay with God; it sometimes seems like forever or that it will never happen for you, but it will because God's time is not our time. With His time and ours, one day is "as a thousand years," (2 Peter 3:8).[36], so you see, you've only been waiting since yesterday. David said, " I waited patiently for the Lord. . ." (Psalms 40:1)[37] so don't get in a hurry. Though it tarry, it will come (Habakkuk 2:3).[38]

How do I know? Because I waited, and it came for me, after seven and a half years of working in the church, being faithful to everything in my local church first, then to the district, the state and the National, taking off of my job every first Thursday so that I could attend every first Thursday Women's fellowship meeting. I would go and just sit there and listen to young women being told we didn't know what we were doing. This made for hurt feelings and many young women my age stopped going and went away wounded by the church. I stayed because I wanted so much to be a part of the work of God in the church. I kept on going, and I made up my mind that I couldn't give up. That's why I decided to write this little book because it just might encourage our young women to know that you are not the only one. I could provide names of many great leaders now who were told, "You don't know what you're doing." Some of us stayed there and I, personally, made a promise to God that I would never let myself become a mean, old, woman being jealous and hateful to women younger than me. I feel blessed to have younger women as my daughters and my sisters. I don't ever want them to feel like they can't talk to me about anything and there are others that I know young women can share with and it won't be in the local news. I know how to keep a secret. So many years, I prayed for someone that I could share my mistakes with who had made mistakes themselves and God helped them come out and they were gracious enough to help me. Unfortunately, I could not tell anybody because it just meant that I would be judged as a young woman not knowing what she was doing, so I just kept it all to myself, trying to please people, trying to win their approval. As I said earlier, daughters, You don't need anybody's approval but God's. Mothers, we need a new approach to help our daughters, or we will never help them or gain their confidence. Mothers, our daughters need someone to talk to who will feel their cares and listen without criticizing and judging them before they hear the whole story. Mothers, let us put ourselves in this place. I don't know about you, but I was one day in that place. I worked for years for the approval of my leaders, but living for God taught me different. I no longer work looking for approval. I work for God's approval. I serve and I give because I love my leaders. Our State Supervisor, in particular, is not judgmental; she is not critical. She tries to carry us all with the program, and she involves every woman, old and young. She gives of her self, and treats us all fair as is humanly possible, so women, young and old, let me borrow from Mother Welch's theme and say that it's time to "Turn the Page." We have stayed on the former page too long. The past two years have been like coming out of the twilight zone. Thank you, Mother

Welch, for sharing your vision with us. I want to be the hotline for our daughters as an older mother. I hope to show something in my life that would cause our daughters to feel like they can talk with me about any problem. It is important to me to make sure that they feel that they can trust me.

CHAPTER TEN

The Blessings of the Lord

I have been talking about the problems, but I also must share the blessings that God has bestowed upon me. I told you about "Mr. Tall, Dark and Handsome" who was a "wolf in sheep's clothing", but my blessing came when I met my James, whom I call "Babe." We met each other not by me looking for him, nor by him looking for me, but God did it for us. We lived over three thousand miles apart and had never heard of each other. Friends of mine were also friends of his; they told him about me and gave him my phone number. Thank God he used it! He called me, told me his name, and asked me to call his mother, who lived in Oakland, Ca. At first, I said, " I don't know your mama!" but he insisted I call her so I did. She invited me to visit her, and I accepted. She cooked dinner for me and while she cooked, I fell asleep on her couch. While I was asleep on this strange woman's couch, I didn't know that James had asked all of his family to come over and "check me out", so when I woke up from my nap, the room was full of strange people whom I had never seen before all looking at me. . . smiling. I was too embarrassed to speak. I didn't know if I had been snoring, drooling with my mouth open or, only the Lord knows what else. I finally got myself together enough to sit up and say "hello" –that was in November 1964. His mother told him I was very friendly because I had fallen asleep on her couch. I guess she felt like I had to be okay if I felt comfortable enough to fall asleep in a total stranger's house. In the latter part of January 1965, he invited me to visit him in Texas. After I cleared it with my pastor and many others, I went to Texas to see him. Up until this point, all I had was a picture of him and he of me. He came to the train station and took me to stay with a preacher friend and his wife. He had his own home, so I went to see where he lived; it was nice. The Lord was truly blessing me. He had a home, a job, a car and was a minister of the Gospel. The same day that I met him for the first time, he put an engagement ring on my finger and asked me to marry him. I asked him to give me five months to pray about it and he agreed. Five months later, on June 12, 1965, my daddy, Elder F. W. Cotton performed the wedding ceremony. That was thirty-seven years, nine months ago and we are still together. We were told by people in both of our church homes that we would not last six months, yet here we are thirty-seven years, nine months later just growing older each day, but I thank God, we are growing together. Because I waited on him, God gave me a husband made just for me. For thirty-five years, I didn't have to cook or shop for groceries. To this day, we wash together and we make up our bed together. Because I didn't settle for less, God gave me the best. Single women wait on God for your mate. Don't let anybody rush you into marriage even if you are accused of being in a lesbian relationship. You know whether or not you are. Most important, God knows. You may even be accused of having a hidden boyfriend that you are seeing. Through it all, hold your head up high and stay with God. I am a witness, he will see you through, and he will send you a companion made just for you. God has no respect of person; if He did it for me back then, He'll do it again. He loves you; God is just waiting on you to admit you have a need and could use his help. Don't you know my daughters, God is our only help? Oh yes, this is where I must tell you it's not going to be "sugar and spice and everything nice." No, there will be some bad times, but it's up to you daughters to make it last. I have a great marriage, but it was not always like that; we had our bad days, but most important, we had God in our lives and all our good times outweighed the bad times. After many years, there are three things that I would like to share with you that will help your marriage. First of all, have a prayer life. Secondly, "zip your lips", and finally, keep the third party out of your marriage unless it's Jesus. Advice that I would add to these three principles would be to never scream at each other unless the house is on fire, never go to sleep without saying "I am sorry" if you have been in an argument and make sure you kiss each other good night. Marriage is "give and take." Both parties have to give some and take some. Daughters, it's up to you to keep your marriages together. If you listen to some of the older women's testimonies, you will understand what I am trying to tell you when I say it's a "give and take." Come to some of our Women's fellowship meetings. I wish you could have been in the California Northwest Worker's meeting in 2003 and the March 1st Monthly Women's Fellowship of 2003. Our State Supervisor, Mother Welch gave her testimony and it was exactly what our young wives needed to hear, so they would know that even if their marriage is a little rocky, they could still be successful if they stay together. It can be done because somebody has already been there and done that. Daughters, strive to keep your families together. After Jesus, there is nothing more important than your family. I always had my family, but a few years ago, I didn't have a very good relationship with them anymore, but I never stopped praying that I would get my family back and I will keep praying for a real family relationship once more with all my family. Young women, this is your time to help us carry the church work on.

CHAPTER ELEVEN

There's a Balm for You

Young women, I must give you hope and you need to know that this is truly your time. It's time for us to get together and find a solution for whatever hurts you are feeling, help for every wound that you have been inflicted with, and, as a mother, I know you have been wounded sometimes by friends, family members, church family members, parents, or even children. However, listen! There is a healing for your wounds, the ones you received from family members, co-workers on your job, your friends, or even members in church. Daughters, stay prayerful because there's a balm for you; there is a Physician for the health of our daughters (Jeremiah 8:22).[39] Love cures all and I do love you, daughters. Mothers, take your daughters along with you and ask them to visit with you. Sit down with them share some your experiences with them; let them know we have faults, and that we have made mistakes in our younger days. Some of us never had an opportunity to make mistakes because we never tried or did anything, even before we got saved. While we were young and now that we are older, we feel like we have missed out on our young life and somewhere inside of us, we are bitter toward our younger daughters. Don't be. Love them and be a mother to them; teach them to be good mothers to their children. Be an example for them and give them a positive model to go by from your life. I read somewhere that an older woman is as a dictionary, and if she dies the meanings for life are gone and lost for the younger women. We go to the dictionary to learn the meaning of words, so let's be a dictionary for our daughters. We must show them the understanding of life from a Godly perspective. Mothers, don't let the devil make you lock up your dictionary; if you do, you will take away the meaning and understanding from our daughters. Mothers, let's "get real."

Our youth are leaving the church looking for an answer and many of them are sick from substance abuse. I read that "9.9 teens, ages 12-17 are trapped by drugs and alcohol."[40] Many of these children are our daughters and sons, grandchildren, great-grandchildren, nieces and nephews. Many of us may not have been hooked on drugs, but we were hooked on something else. My "vice" was cigarettes before the Lord saved me. I smoked three packs in a day and night, and I couldn't help myself. I was addicted to blues, and I thought I had to have a BC standback, a powder that could be bought over the counter at the drug store, and a Coke; I couldn't get through the day without one. I would buy a coke and this substance. I was truly hooked! Some of you probably haven't heard of this "over-the- counter" drug; it was a headache medication, and I was just as addicted to that as someone on cocaine. See, so I can't "point the finger" at anyone, but I can recommend a cure: get saved and filled with the Holy Ghost and you won't even have to use methadone to taper off the addiction. Just get full of the Word of God and there won't be room for habits of any kind.

CHAPTER TWELVE

Passing The Baton

Mothers, we must prepare our youth to carry the church on. Our days are coming to an end; one day soon, somebody will have to take our place; the only way that we can do that is that we must help them now. All young people are not unsaved, just like all older people are not unsaved, so why shouldn't we get together and work for the good of God? Let us not give up on our youth; we need them and they need us. With so much trouble in our world today: wars and rumors of wars and nations against nations, it's time for us as the people of God to stop fighting one another and begin fighting the devil who is stealing our young people. Come on mother, let's get together, and take back our power, our strength, and our faith and trust, knowing that our God can do anything. Together we stand and divided we fall. Come on Mothers, let's bring our daughters into the fold and teach them about the traps of the devil and show them the goodness of God.

We must let them know that there is a better life. Somebody showed us a better way; we were once young and now we are old, but we can let our daughters know if they live right; they will never have to stoop to the devil. God will supply all their need... (Philippians 4:19).[41] We must find a way and time to teach this by precept and example. In other words, sharing our real living experiences will help our daughters through their difficult times. As I discussed earlier, I lived with a total income of two hundred and fifty dollars, but because I trusted in the Lord, he took care of me and my children; He blessed me to work for good people who helped me go to nursing school to get a better job. I know it was all in God's plan for me. I didn't understand at the time; I had many foolish questions such as "Why me, Lord?" and "Why did I give up a good man for this?" You may be asking yourself these questions. Well, let me give you some answers. I got my answers from God; it was praying and waiting. I prayed and put my request in the prayer box at my home church, Faith Temple Church of God in Christ. My request was answered when the Lord sent me, my James, which is my babe. Listen daughters, God loves you and he will do the same thing if you believe him: he will do whatever you believe Him to do. I remember Bishop Hamilton, the bishop for California Northwest Ecclesiastical Jurisdiction (CNW), was the guest speaker for the Greater Emmanuel District in the CNW jurisdiction. The meeting took place at the Emmanuel Church of God in Christ in San Francisco. His message was "How to Bring the Glory Back: get the Church Back Together." (Oh,

Thank God!). Souls were blessed and the anointing of God was present in the room. Do you remember when miracles were wrought right before our eyes? That was what we could feel in the room that day. My heart filled with great joy and I added when we pray, repent and humble ourselves, look for his face and stop our wicked ways; he will listen and send the glory back. I want the glory back: that confidence and power will work again in our churches. People will be healed, saved and filled with the Holy Ghost. Bishop Hamilton said, "we sing the song, 'I Wish Somebody's Soul Would Catch on Fire and Burn with the Holy Ghost'[42], and as soon as thy catch on fire, we grab a fire hose and put it out." I added, the fire hose we use, mothers, is "sit her down because her dress is too short, too tight, she's got on pants or throw a sheet over her." Well that will surely put the fire out. Let the Lord work because God will not cause anybody to be ashamed; God wants us to go back to the old landmark and take our youth with us. Proverbs 30:32 tells us, "if thou hast done foolishly in lifting up thyself, or if thou hast thought evil lay thine hand upon thy mouth."[43] We need to pray more for our youth and stop thinking evil because all youth are not on drugs; they are looking for answers. They are pleading for help from us since we seem to have all the answers about everything. We are coming through but how? They want and need an example, not talk. We need to admit that we have done many things foolishly in trying to lead our daughters down the same path we took . We should strive to show them the Bible way and not our traditions or what used to be or the way we did "it." It's not about us; it's all about Jesus and bringing souls to Him.

On Monday night, March 3, 2003, I went to a District Meeting where Mother Welch was the speaker. Her scripture was taken from Psalms 137:1-4[44] and Psalms 63:1-2.[45] The power of God filled the room; the anointing was with Mother Welch and we could feel the presence of God all over the building. This is what the people need. We need the Latter rain. Lord, send the Latter rain; send the power; send the glory and give us understanding of how to work with the youth of this day. We must stay spiritual and not compromise the Word of God. We must restore our youth in a spirit of meekness considering ourselves. I am sure that our leaders, when I was young, wondered to themselves, " what kind of children have we let into our church?" We didn't dress the way they did, but there were some that loved us enough and could see the worth in us and knew God's hands was on us for a greater work. After they had gone to be with the Lord, to name a few My daddy, Superintendent F.W. Cotton, Superintendent B.B. Alexander, Mother Young, Mother McGlothen, Bishop S.R. Martin, Mother L. Perrodin, and Mother Thompson of San Mateo, I could hear them telling us to "come out of that corner, you can't hide, God sent me to tell you, you can't hide; the searchlight's on",[46] but they did it with wisdom and brought more souls to Christ then I could even name. Bishop E.E. the father of the Family of California Northwest and Mother Bessie, the first lady of California Northwest taught me many things that I treasure today. Now, Mothers let us strive to leave some footprints in the sands for our daughters to follow. I remember when they told me my clothes were too short for the church. Some told me with a mean voice, but there was Mother Louise Perrodin who came to me and said, "Baby, you look pretty, but please, I want you to come to my house and I will help you make it a little longer." Today, I wear my skirts longer because of the way she approached me. Mothers it's our approach that makes the difference with our daughters. Let's make that difference and make our youth a part of the church and they won't leave us.

CHAPTER THIRTEEN

It's Not an Outside Need; It's an Inside Need

The devil has played a real trick on us; some of us got saved and because we had family members not saved, we separated ourselves from them and didn't realize this was breaking up our families; it takes families to make up the church; that's why our churches are empty. Let's go get our families and bring them to church with us no matter what they are wearing because it's not an outside need; it's an inside need. The Holy Ghost will lead and guide you into all things, (John 16:13)[47] that means how to dress, how to walk, and how to talk. We didn't dress right until it got in our hearts; some of us are wearing everything to church so maybe they are looking at us and saying I don't like what you wear to church, which means that we must look at ourselves and try to remember that this is a two way street. No one drives alone; there's always somebody on the same road and sometimes there's road construction. Because of the construction, you must make many detours to get where you are going, but if you follow directions which is the Bible, you get there. Just always remember that you are not the only one on the road; where there is construction, you some times have to go out of your way to get to your destination; there are many road blocks in our spiritual walk with God. Be assured, God always gives us a detour, so let's go another mile to help our youth of today; it is our duty and our responsibility to win souls for Christ. The church is at a crossroads; we must make a decision to look for the old paths and walk therein or we will never find rest for our souls (Jeremiah 6:16).[48] If we begin to say, "we will not walk therein", this world is restless and troublesome, everywhere, but there is some real peace found in God. Mothers, sisters and brothers, we can bring that peace through prayer together. The jails are filled with our sons and daughters; war clouds are hanging over our heads; our children are dying on the streets. Without God, it's time for us to take the Gospel to the streets. We must leave the comfort zone; we say that this generation is lost. Well, who is to blame? Let us get together and go find them and show them the way to Jesus. Let's take them back to holiness; it's time to stop playing church, compromising the Gospel and really make soul winning our main focus.

I was called by God to be an evangelist, thirty-five years ago. Someone might be wondering why it took me so long to really do God's will. Well, let me tell you. I let people make me ashamed and afraid to do His will, but at this time in my life, I am asking God to forgive me and give me another chance to obey his will not man's. I am lifting my hands up, meaning I am fully surrendered to God, to obey His will. From this day forward, I will be the obedient, God-fearing, bold, unashamed servant of God; I can't teach our daughters to have faith and surrender to the will of God in everything if I don't do it myself, so Mothers let us begin to live and teach what we preach; let them know it's not just talk. We have friends, family members, extended family and church family members who have been wounded in the church and don't want to come back, but we must bring them back and the only way we will be able to do this is that we, first, must lift up Jesus and He will draw.

Not only have our young daughters and single women been wounded, but widows are hurting as well. There are widows, old and young sitting at home feeling like nobody cares; maybe that's not how it is, but we are responsible for their souls, so today be a good Samaritan; go and wrap up those wounds and take up those who have been wounded in the church (Luke 10:33-34).[49] Those out of the arc of safety need a lifeline; let us throw it out before they drift away.

CHAPTER FOURTEEN

Promotion Comes from God

There are sisters and brothers, sons and daughters who feel that nobody cares because they didn't get the position they thought they should have gotten. Listen, my dears, promotion comes not from the east, north, south or west, but it comes from God and when He puts you up, no man can take you down, so those of you that's sitting home feeling like you have been hurt by others, stop and think. You will see that you have hurt yourself by working for the approval of people; open your eyes and look around you and you will see how much work there is to be done and how many souls there are to be won. Forget about yourself and set your sights on Jesus. Stop having pity parties; don't invite "usta"; don't invite in "my day." That's gone. We are in a new day with a great job to do for Christ. We have no time to sit at home reminiscing about what we use to do or what somebody didn't let us do. God gave you the job; He's your boss so nobody can stop you, but you, as I told you earlier. I mentioned before, envy, jealousy, unforgiveness on the inside is like a sore with a scab over it; it will always hurt until it is debrided and the puss is able to run out. Unless you forgive and ask for forgiveness, you will have a nasty, ugly sore covered with a scab that hurts all the time and it won't heal until you let all the puss drain out; then, and only then, will it heal from the inside out. There are times when a scar is left, but you are healed, so come on Mothers and Fathers, let us debride the sores. We have been carrying for years Jealously, Hatred, Envy, being angry at the world, and being angry at the church because we have let the devil tell us that we weren't treated right because we were here "first." Mothers, you have been telling yourself, "I should have been the church mother", "I should have been the District Missionary, but they passed over me", or even "I should have been the State Supervisor." Oh, how sad! Look at yourself, then ask yourself a question: "Was I prepared for this position spiritually? Could I have made the sacrifice it takes to be in these positions?" "Was it God's will?" We must ask ourselves, "Is it in God's plan for me? Have I acknowledged him in this matter?" He said in Proverbs 3:6, "In all thy ways acknowledge Him and He shall direct thy paths."[50] Find a friend or most important be a friend; find time to help someone along the way and I promise, you won't find so much time to feel sorry for yourself; be a big Sister, or a mother; do something for others; don't let your life consist of just "you and your four and no more." Many of us have never had to face the devil head on; we have never been caught in a close place with temptation like "Mr. Tall, Dark and Handsome", where you had to make a decision right then to save your spiritual life: I have. But, today, as I write these words, I am grateful and very thankful to the Holy Ghost, who will lead you and guide you into all truth, (John 16:13)[51] if you listen. By the help of God, I am here today to say that I am glad I did listen and did not yield to temptation. Sisters and Brothers, if you have never been in this place where you had to run from temptation, you will never feel the pain for your sisters and brothers who have been found in a fault. Consider yourself. Only Jesus knows when we are ready for that which he has entrusted to us for His use. Don't put confidence in yourself, thinking you can stop whenever you are ready; your are fooling yourself. You are in denial just like an alcoholic walking around drunk all day and saying to himself, " I can quit anytime I get ready." Oh, no you can't. Some of you have been in love affairs with someone whom you have loved, but they have not loved you back, but it's a whole new ball game when you love and you are loved back. It's hard to walk away, and the only way out for you is by letting Jesus fully deliver you. As my daddy said, Elder F.W. Cotton, "you better hear me; you are headed for trouble; that fellow is no good." I love my daddy in his grave for all he taught me. Sisters, learn to love yourself and others will too. Respect yourself, and others will respect you. Always remember you are somebody in the Lord. Today, there are so many problems, heartaches, and painful times. Teenagers, young adults, middle aged adults and older adults feel like more money, more drugs, a bigger house, a new car, a new Mr. Tall, Dark and Handsome is the way to go. Their mind and body tells them that these things are what they need. In other words, that's the "it" that they need. That's not "it" at all. It's your soul that's hungry and thirsty for the living God. "As the hart panteth after the water brook, so panteth my soul after thee, oh God. My soul thirsteth for God, the Living God (Psalm 42:1-2).[52]

CHAPTER FIFTEEN

It's Praying Time

As I come to the end of this little book, I am thanking God for each word He has put into my mouth. I pray to God that some daughter, some mother, some boy or girl will be blessed after reading these words. Let us all change our course of direction and start letting God direct our paths. Love your leaders, especially our pastors and treat them right, and by far, in everything, let's not loose our youth because they don't dress like us, they don't sing our songs like we do. Don't criticize them; take the time to teach them with love, kindness and compassion, always remembering yourselves. Where would we be if Jesus had not touched the heart of some mother to pray for us? Mothers, do you realize that women prayed out the church? I ask for your prayers for our leaders male and female, from local to international. Pray for the leaders of our nation and remember no matter what's going on around us, God is yet in control. Now Mothers and Fathers, if we are ever going to reach this generation, we have got to get out the deep freeze and let the Holy Ghost thaw us out of our insulting views. Let God open our understanding to a more meaningful way to reach our youth, men and women who we need to carry on the work of God. The time is now to train our young women; don't just let them go out there: prepare them for the spiritual war that we must all join together, as one, in, in order to obtain the victory. Mothers, the fight is on; the battle is hot, but there is victory in Christ Jesus. Let us join our hearts together in prayer for this nation. Don't be angry at life for things you didn't do; don't hold bitterness in your heart at those persons who have enjoyed life twice; some of us have lived life to its fullest while we were not saved, and now we live for God with all that's in us. That's what keeps me happy because the world doesn't owe me anything. I am happy with Jesus alone. I hope when you have finished this little book, you will have something in it to keep you encouraged to go on and keep your hope alive. Again, let us join our hearts and thoughts and pray for our leaders and for each other. My prayer is that is some small way, you have found hope in something that I have said. God Bless you and to God Be the Glory.

Endnotes

Introduction

1. King James Version. *The Key Word Study Bible.* Chattanooga: AMG, 1984, 1991, pg. 1447.
2. Ibid. pg. 585.
3. Ibid. pg. 933.
4. Ibid. pg. 798.
5. Ibid. pg. 1477
6. Ibid. pg. 1228.
7. Ibid. pg. 1470.

Chapter One

1. King James Version. *The Key Word Study Bible.* Chattanooga:AMG, 1984, 1991, pg. 1525.
2. Ibid. pg. 1186.

3. Ibid. pg. 1404.

4. Ibid. pg. 1406.

5. Ibid. pg. 1186.

Chapter Three

6. King James Version. *The Key Word Study Bible.* Chattanooga: AMG, 1984, 1991, pg. 1209.

7. Ibid. pg. 678.

8. Ibid. pg. 966.

9. Ibid. pg. 803.

10. Ibid. pg. 1547.

11. Ibid. pg. 1534.

Chapter Four

12. King James Version. *The Key Word Study Bible.* Chattanooga: AMG, 1984, 1991, pg. 1528.

13. Ibid. pg. 1475.

14. Ibid. pg. 1496

15. Ibid. pg. 1447.

16. Ibid. pg. 1184.

17. Ibid. pg. 1185.

Chapter Five

18. King James Version. *The Key Word Study Bible.* Chattanooga: AMG, 1984, 1991, pg. 796.

19. Ibid. pg. 727.

20. Ibid. pg. 781-2.
21. Ibid. pg. 1338.
22. Ibid. pg. 1431.
23. Ibid. pg. 1461.
24. Ibid. pg. 1274.
25. Ibid. pg. 1467.
26. Ibid. pg. 1467.
27. Ibid. pg. 1488.
28. Ibid. pg. 1505.

Chapter Six

29. King James Version. *The Key Word Study Bible.* Chattanooga: AMG, 1984, 1991, pg. 1525.
30. Ibid. pg. 1476.
31. Ibid. pg. 1142.

Chapter Seven

32. King James Version. *The Key Word Study Bible.* Chattanooga: AMG, 1984, 1991, pg. 1508.
33. Ibid. pg. 1508.
34. Public Domain. *Let Us Run to Jesus.*

Chapter Eight

35. King James Version. *The Key Word Study Bible.* Chattanooga: AMG, 1984, 1991, pg. 1412.
36. Ibid. pg. 1545.

37. Ibid. pg. 733.
38. Ibid. pg. 1144.

Chapter Eleven

39. Ibid. pg. 933.
40. Harmon, Cedric. "Champions of Faith. The Man with a Plan." <u>Charisma Magazine</u>. July 2002. **http://www.Charismamag.com**.

Chapter Twelve

41. King James Version. *The Key Word Study Bible.* Chattanooga: AMG, 1984, 1991, pg. 1477.
42. Public Domain. "I Wish Somebody's Soul Would Catch on Fire."
43. King James Version. *The Key Word Study Bible.* Chattanooga: AMG, 1984, 1991, pg. 831.
44. Ibid. pg. 793-4.
45. Ibid. pg. 746.

Chapter Thirteen

46. Public Domain. "Come Out of That Corner."
47. King James Version. *The Key Word Study Bible.* Chattanooga: AMG, 1984, 1991, pg. 1344.
48. Ibid. pg. 929.
49. Ibid. pg. 1284.

Chapter Fourteen

50. King James Version. *The Key Word Study Bible.* Chattanooga: AMG, 1984, 1991, pg. 803.

51. Ibid. pg. 1344.

52. Ibid. pg. 735.

www.ingramcontent.com/pod-product-compliance
Ingram Content Group UK Ltd.
Pitfield, Milton Keynes, MK11 3LW, UK
UKHW041956230426
12048UKWH00008B/367